Written down in pencil

Written down in pencil

by

Sue Lewis

First published 2024 by The Hedgehog Poetry Press,

5 Coppack House, Churchill Avenue, Clevedon. BS21 6QW

www.hedgehogpress.co.uk

ISBN: 978-1-916830-15-8

Contents

for my muse

CHIAROSCURO

I will write to you

& it will be
black night white moon

unfathomably bright

a moon to
hold your breath by

sky punched through with light

beneath the stars
the vixen shadow

yew tree silhouette

quiet unfold of
owl-soft feathers

cat's unweighted tread

let this be the backdrop –
poetry's midnight space

a landscape
holding nothing less

than all we long to say.

KAIROS

Sometimes

after windswept phases
there is healing salt

the moon's serenity
will pour into the street

and for a moment

you'll be startled by your insight

how the taste of it seems
scarlet in your mouth.

Rare grace
to brush against that music

touch the tenderness
of transient things.

NO WAY

Each morning
sun and shade

I open up my window

pierced by birdsong
somewhere else

some days the brilliance
is all that I can see
my garden
a philanthropy of green

but in the kitchen

white tiles
slowly ticking clocks
a dresser full of empty plates

my words are nothing

scratches on a wall.

CRUSH

This wardrobe holds
our things unsaid

its doors can barely close

there are so many versions
all in different shades

but I have shut them in

most are for everyday
(well, you have seen all those)

but these mute colours

moon-washed   untranslatable

I dare not let you see.

TIME

is a dandelion clock

raised up on bitter milk

proud, perfect orb
self-confident beneath the sun

brief fragile sphere
ghost-feathered globe

soft-spiked unstable bomb
which breeze can detonate

or breath can kiss
to bless each seed with love

before its pilgrimage
towards infinity.

INTERVENTION

Bright covering of light
disturbance
of the status quo

not this
not that

but something on your mind

we will not say
that you are on your knees

but

through the spice of perfumed air
there is a half-remembered tune
trapped in the fabric
apt to take a darker tone.

Within the absence
often
something brave will fail

don't be afraid
angels will come

much later

you may recognise them.

FALLEN

The angel
that I found in you
turned bad

heaven knows
how this will end

I would have knelt
forever at your feet

you had that shine

now you, too,
have shown
your base metal

and I must raise
my flaming sword
to keep you out

tell me
why does everything
need expression

we should have
stayed in that garden

because I miss you

all the same, I miss you.

DON'T EAT THE SEEDS

for winter always wants
to drag you back

black months
when shadows
take on terrifying shapes

dark streets are mazed
and barren

angles blurred
in that half-light

the stone-faced moon
quite pitiless:

don't enter that abyss

but wait upon the spring
and sun your fragile wings
upon my windowsill

grow tall again
under a faultless sky

he took your joy
obscured your shine

I never liked him.

DUET

Within this
wood-warm place of peace

bright antique music
weaves and separates

fills up the circle of the room
and gathers at the apex of the roof

where one tall window
holds the sun

and frames high branches
patient in the April light.

Bare twigs
about to burst with song.

SET PIECE

Under a lily sky
we stumble into grief

dark crows
stab the meadow

painful daylight
grass scorched gold

burnt exhausted summer
trees already thinning

the spaces in between

what's not said
what's not there

the missing; the missing

written down in pencil
carelessly erased

absent from this painting

only shadows stay.

SOMETHING YOU ONCE SAID

about the sweet release of music;
how concentrating sets us free

how moonlight speaks a different language;
how we feel those soft moth wings of fear

that out of shot is chaos;
how memory's a cloak of gaps

how on my sun-white windowsill –
first butterfly of spring

how dusk can shrink a lonely room
and thin the space between us

and how we settle for the calm of it:

evening colours

birdsong

the quiet turning of a page.

UNFOLDED

I open for you
like a map

unfold myself
spread out

reveal my creases
contours

weather faded
water marked

old colours
subtle, beautiful

rare chart
of days and hours

of sun and stars
and shadows

meadows, mountains
forests, seas

and all of these
I share with you

for nothing
must be lost

each place
a welcome home

each precious line
a journey

not quite over yet.

INSUFFICIENT MUSIC

After fine days
one by one

an evening storm
will break:

wet grass
bruised sky

grief spills between my fingers

takes me by surprise

the unstopped clock
still beats

your voice still faint
inside your letters

ghost within
my photographs

but there is
insufficient music
to erase

this howl
of quiet finality.

ACKNOWLEDGEMENTS

With grateful thanks to all my fellow writers in Poets Anonymous, Sutton Writers, Mole Valley Poets, Leaves to a Tree and the Tuesday/Friday Poets. Your solidarity, encouragement and guidance is so important to me. And thank you, Mark, at Hedgehog Press for having faith in my poems and giving them a voice.